# Succeed on the NJ ASK

## This Book Includes:

- 3 NJ ASK Practice tests similar to the actual test
- Detailed answer explanations for every question
- In-depth coverage of multiple-choice, Short Constructed Response and Extended Constructed Response questions
- Strategies for building speed and accuracy
- Aligned with the new Common Core State Standards

## Plus One Year access to Online Workbooks

- Hundreds of practice questions
- Individualized score reports
- Instant feedback after completion of the workbook
- Students can complete the Online Workbooks at their own pace

## Complement Classroom Learning All Year

Using the Lumos Study Program, parents and teachers can reinforce the classroom learning experience for children. It creates a collaborative learning platform for students, teachers and parents.

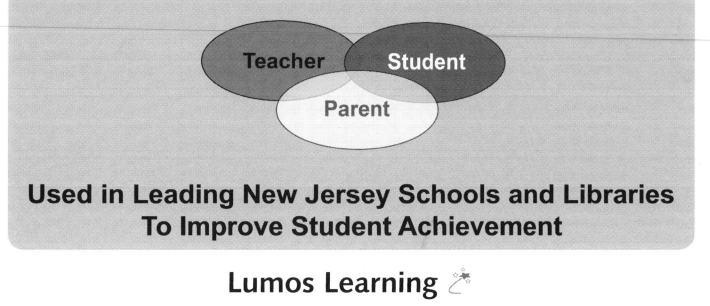

## Used in Leading New Jersey Schools and Libraries To Improve Student Achievement

## Lumos Learning

# NJ ASK Practice Tests and Online Workbooks: Grade 6 Mathematics, Second Edition

**Contributing Editor**          - JennyLynn Carey
**Contributing Editor**          - Gregory Applegate
**Contributing Editor**          - Margaret Provenzano
**Executive Producer**           - Mukunda Krishnaswamy
**Designer and Illustrator**     - Mirona Jova

ISBN-13: 978-1479223503

ISBN-10: 1479223506
Printed in the United States of America

## For permissions and additional information contact us

Lumos Information Services, LLC
PO Box 1575, Piscataway, NJ 08855-1575
http://www.lumostestprep.com

Email: support@lumostestprep.com
Tel: (732) 384-0146
Fax: (866)283-6471

# Lumos Learning

# Table of Contents

# Introduction

The New Jersey Assessment of Skills and Knowledge (NJ ASK) is a comprehensive standards-based assessment administered in the New Jersey schools every year. Student success on this test has significant benefits to all stake holders – students, parents, teachers, and school administration. Success on this test requires students to demonstrate good test taking skills and competency in all key areas covered in the Common Core State Standards.

**How can students succeed on the NJ ASK through this Lumos Study Program?**
At Lumos Learning, we believe that yearlong learning and adequate practice before the actual test are the keys to student success on the NJ ASK. We have designed the Lumos NJ ASK Study Program to help students get plenty of realistic practice before the test and to promote yearlong collaborative learning.

Inside this book, you will find **three full-length practice tests** that are similar to the NJ ASK. Completing these tests will help students master the different areas that are included in the new Common Core State Standards and practice test taking skills. The results will help the students and educators get insights into students' strengths and weaknesses in particular content areas. These insights could be used to help students strengthen their skills in difficult topics and to improve speed and accuracy while taking the test.

The Lumos NJ ASK **Online Workbooks** are designed to promote yearlong learning. It is a simple program students can access using a computer with internet access in a secure manner. It consists of hundreds of grade appropriate questions based on the new Common Core State Standards. Students will get instant feedback and can review their answers anytime. Each student's answers and progress can be reviewed by parents and educators to reinforce the learning experience.

LumosTestPrep.com

# How to use this book effectively

The Lumos NJ ASK Study Program is a flexible learning tool. It can be adapted to suit a student's skill level and the time available to practice before the NJ ASK. Here are some tips to help you use this book and the online workbooks effectively:

## Students
- You can use the "Diagnostic Test" to understand your mastery of different topics and test taking skills.
- Use the "Related Lumos Online Workbook" in the Answer Key section to identify the topic that is related to each question.
- Use the Online workbooks to practice your areas of difficulty and complement class room learning.
- Have Extended Constructed responses evaluated by a teacher or parent keeping in mind the scoring rubrics.
- Take the "Practice Tests" as you get close to the NJ ASK test date.
- Complete the test in a quiet place, following the test guidelines. Practice tests provide you an opportunity to improve your test taking skills and to review topics included in the NJ ASK test.

## Parents
- Familiarize yourself with the test format and expectations.
- Help your child use Lumos Online Workbooks by following the instructions in "How to access the Lumos Online Workbooks" section of this chapter.
- Review your child's performance in the "Lumos Online Workbooks" periodically. You can do this by simply asking your child to log into the system online and selecting the subject area you wish to review.

Review your child's work in the Practice Tests. To get a sense of how the Extended Constructed questions are graded review scoring rubrics online at http://www.state.nj.us/education/assessment/es

## Teachers
- Please contact **support@lumoslearning.com** to request a **teacher account**. A teacher account will help you create custom assessments and lessons as well as review the online work of your students.
- Visit **http://www.lumoslearning.com/math-quill** to learn more.
- If your school has purchased the school edition of this book, please use this book as the Teacher Guide.
- You can use the Lumos online programs along with this book to complement and extend your classroom instruction.

# NJ ASK Frequently Asked Questions

## What is the NJ ASK?

It is an acronym for the standardized test administered in the New Jersey public schools (New Jersey Assessment of Skills and Knowledge). It is given every year to students in grades 3 through 8. Students in Grade 6 are tested in Mathematics and Language Arts Literacy. NJ ASK scores are reported as scale scores in each content area. The scores range from 100-199 (Partially Proficient), 200-249 (Proficient) and 250-300 (Advanced Proficient).

## When is the NJ ASK given?

It is normally administered in the spring. Please obtain the exact dates of your test from your school.

## What is the format of the NJ ASK?

The NJ ASK Math consists of 35 Multiple-Choice questions, 6 Short Constructed Response (SCR) questions and 3 Extended Constructed Response (ECR) questions.
For Extended Constructed questions, students are asked to construct written responses, in their own words. Each test section needs to be completed in the allotted time. Test administrators ensure that students adhere to the test guidelines.

## What is the duration of the test?

Grade 6 students take the NJ ASK over a four day period. The first two days are devoted to the Language Arts Literacy test and the next two days to the Mathematics test. On each of the test days students spend from 60 to 100 minutes working on the test.

## Where can I get additional information about the NJ ASK?

You can obtain a lot of useful information about the test, schedules and performance reports by visiting the New Jersey State Department of Education's website at
http://www.state.nj.us/education/assessment/

## Where can I get additional information about the Common Core State Standards (CCSS)?

Please visit http://www.corestandards.org/Math

# How to access the Lumos Online Workbooks

**First Time Access:**
Using a computer with internet access, go to
http://www.lumostestprep.com/book

Select the name of your book from the book selection drop-down menu.

| | |
|---|---|
| Book | Grade 6 Math ▾ |
| Book Access Code: | |
| | Enter |

Enter the following access code in the Access Code field and press the Enter button.

Access Code: 7512259441

In the next screen, click on the "New User" button to register your user name and password.

**Subsequent Access:**

**Welcome NJ ASK Grade 6 Math Book Customer!**

If you are a New User, please register.

| | |
|---|---|
| Login | |
| Password | |
| | Enter |

After you establish your user id and password for subsequent access, simply login with your account information.

### What if I have access to more than one Lumos Study Program?

Please note that you can access all Online Workbooks using one user id and password. If your organization has purchased subscription to more than one Lumos Study Program book, simply follow the instruction above for First Time Access for the first book. Please work on at least one workbook before you exit.

Go back to the http://www.lumostestprep.com/book link and select the second book from the book selection drop-down menu. Enter the access code in the Access Code field provided in the second book. In the next screen simply login using your previously created account.

# Test Taking Tips

1) **The day before the test**, make sure you get a good night's sleep.
2) **On the day of the test**, be sure to eat a good hearty breakfast! Also, be sure to arrive at school on-time.
3) **During the test:**

   Read every question carefully.

   While Answering Multiple-Choice questions:
   - Do not circle the answer choices. Fill in the bubble corresponding to your answer choice.
   - Read **all** of the answer choices, even if think you have found the correct answer.
   - Do not spend too much time on any one question. Work steadily through all questions in the section.
   - Attempt all of the questions even if you are not sure of some answers.
   - If you run into a difficult question, eliminate as many choices as you can and then pick the best one of the remaining choices. Intelligent guessing will help you increase your score.
   - Also, mark the question so that if you have extra time, you can return to it after you reach the end of the section. Try to erase the marks after you complete the work.
   - Some questions may refer to a graph, chart, or other kind of picture. Carefully review the graphic before answering the question.

   While Answering Open-ended questions:
   - Open-ended questions typically have multiple parts. Make sure you answer **all** parts clearly.
   - Be sure to include explanations for your written responses and show all work.
   - Some questions may refer to a graph, chart, or other kind of picture. Carefully review the graphic before answering the question.

LumosTestPrep.com

# Diagnostic Test

## Part A

Here are some reminders for when you are taking the multiple-choice section.

- Carefully read each problem before choosing an answer.
- Be sure to choose only one answer for each problem.
- Do not spend too much time on any one problem. If you are having difficulty with a problem, skip it and move on to the next problem.
- You can come back to the skipped problem later if you have time.

1. Which of these is the standard form of twenty and sixty-three thousandths?

Ⓐ 20.63000
Ⓑ 20.0063
Ⓒ 20.63
Ⓓ 20.063

2. Which of the following statements is true?

Ⓐ Perpendicular lines must cross, but intersecting lines do not have to cross.
Ⓑ Perpendicular lines never cross, but intersecting lines always cross.
Ⓒ Perpendicular lines must cross to form ninety degree angles, but intersecting lines cross to form angles of varying measures.
Ⓓ Perpendicular lines must cross to form obtuse angles, whereas intersecting lines must cross to form acute angles.

3. When two fractions with different denominators are to be added using the standard procedure, which of these must first be found?

Ⓐ The GCF (Greatest Common Factor) of the fractions
Ⓑ The prime factorization of the fractions' numerators
Ⓒ The LCD (Least Common Denominator) of the fractions
Ⓓ The mean value of the denominators

4. Which fraction below is greater than $\frac{3}{5}$ but less than $\frac{3}{4}$?

    Ⓐ $\frac{1}{3}$

    Ⓑ $\frac{5}{8}$

    Ⓒ $\frac{1}{2}$

    Ⓓ $\frac{4}{5}$

5. 50 percent of 65 is approximately equal to _____ .

    Ⓐ 15
    Ⓑ 25
    Ⓒ 30
    Ⓓ 40

6. Which of the following is not a quadrilateral?

    Ⓐ Square
    Ⓑ Triangle
    Ⓒ Trapezoid
    Ⓓ Rhombus

7. Which of the following sets below contains only prime numbers?

    Ⓐ 7, 11, 49
    Ⓑ 7, 37, 51
    Ⓒ 7, 23, 47
    Ⓓ 2, 29, 93

8. Which of the following statements is not true?

    Ⓐ The denominator is the bottom number in a fraction.
    Ⓑ The multiples of 9 are 1, 3, and 9.
    Ⓒ The factors of 12 are 1, 2, 3, 4, 6, and 12.
    Ⓓ A mixed number consists of a whole number and a fraction.

LumosTestPrep.com

9. When the expression 3(n + 7) is evaluated for a given value of n, the result is 33. What is the value of n?

$$3(4+7) = 33$$

   Ⓐ n = 4
   Ⓑ n = 5
   Ⓒ n = 21
   Ⓓ n = 120

10. The city of Trenton hired a crew of 100 workers to clean up the streets of the city. The crew worked for 14 days. Each worker was paid at a rate of $90 per day. What was the total labor cost for the city?

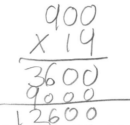

   Ⓐ $1,260
   Ⓑ $126,000
   Ⓒ $11,400
   Ⓓ $9,000

11. The measure of an angle is approximately 105 degrees. What type of angle is it?

   Ⓐ Right
   Ⓑ Acute
   Ⓒ Obtuse
   Ⓓ Oblong

12. Simplify the following ratio:

$$\frac{4}{22}$$

   Ⓐ $\frac{1}{11}$

   Ⓑ $\frac{2}{11}$

   Ⓒ $\frac{8}{44}$

   Ⓓ $\frac{3}{21}$

13. What would be the next two numbers in the following sequence?

   1600, 800, 400, ____ , ____

   Ⓐ 500, 600
   Ⓑ 200, 100
   Ⓒ 200, 0
   Ⓓ 0, -400

14. Joyce is putting a decorative border below the ceiling of her bedroom. The bedroom's ceiling is a rectangle. The shorter sides are 12 feet and the longer sides are 16 feet. What is the perimeter of the ceiling?

Ⓐ 192 ft.
Ⓑ 28 ft.
Ⓒ 56 ft.
Ⓓ 768 ft.

$2 \times 12 =$

$+ \; 2 \times 16 =$

15. Solve: x - 4 < 5

Ⓐ x > 9
Ⓑ x < 9
Ⓒ x > 1
Ⓓ x < 1

**Questions 16 and 17 are short constructed response questions.**

• Carefully read each problem before writing your answer.

16. At the county fair, a small drink costs 75 cents. Lisa and her three friends each buy a small drink. They pay with a five-dollar bill. How much change should they receive?

17. If the total number of faces on a triangular pyramid is subtracted from the total number of faces on a cube, what is the result?

# Extended Constructed Response 1

Here are some reminders for when you are completing this Extended Constructed Response task.

- Carefully read each part of the task before writing your response on a sheet of paper.
- Be sure to complete all parts of the task.
- Clearly explain your answer and show all your work.
- Your explanation can include words, tables, diagrams, or pictures.
- You may use a calculator and a ruler for this task.

The Note-Worthy Music Shop sells CD's in its store locations for $13.00 each. They are trying to attract online buyers by offering deals through their website. CD's purchased online cost $10.00 each. For online purchases, there is a one-time processing fee of $2.50, and a shipping fee of $1.50 per order.

Use the above information to complete the following:

The cost to buy n CD's in the store could be found using:

C = $13.00(n)

Write an equation that could be used to find the cost of n CD's purchased online.

If a customer wanted to buy 8 CD's, which method would be a better choice? Explain your answer using information from the problem.

LumosTestPrep.com

# Work area for Extended Constructed Response 1

# Part B

18. If these six cards were placed into a bag, what would be the probability of randomly choosing a card with "F" or "N"?

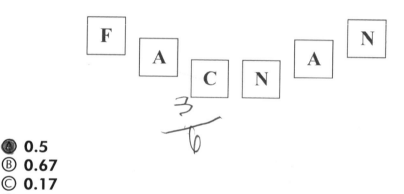

$$\frac{3}{6}$$

Ⓐ 0.5
Ⓑ 0.67
Ⓒ 0.17
Ⓓ 0.33

19. Which one of these proportions is true?

Ⓐ $\frac{3}{5} = \frac{7}{11}$

Ⓑ $\frac{9}{6} = \frac{15}{10}$

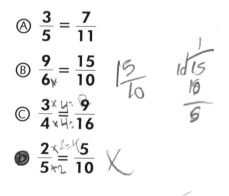

Ⓒ $\frac{3}{4} = \frac{9}{16}$

Ⓓ $\frac{2}{5} = \frac{5}{10}$ ✗

20. Write an equivalent expression to 12x+3.

Ⓐ 12(x+1)
Ⓑ 3(4x + 1)
Ⓒ 6(2x-2)
Ⓓ 3(9x+1)

21. Leonardo and six friends want to go mountain biking. They will all meet at Dale's house, load the bikes into cars, and then drive to the trail. What information do they need to consider as they plan their trip?

Ⓐ The brand of bike owned by each rider
Ⓑ The number of bikes each car can carry
Ⓒ The top speed of each bike
Ⓓ The age of each member of the group

22. Which of the following measurements requires the highest degree of accuracy?

Ⓐ The distance a kindergarten student walks home every day
Ⓑ The dimensions of the window frame to replace a broken pane
Ⓒ The amount of time you spend completing each math problem, if twenty problems were assigned
Ⓓ The size and weight of your bicycle after you fill the tires with air

23. Which of the figures below is not a regular polygon?

Ⓐ

Ⓑ

Ⓒ

Ⓓ

**24.** What is the measure of the third interior angle in this triangle?

*There are 180° In a Triangle*

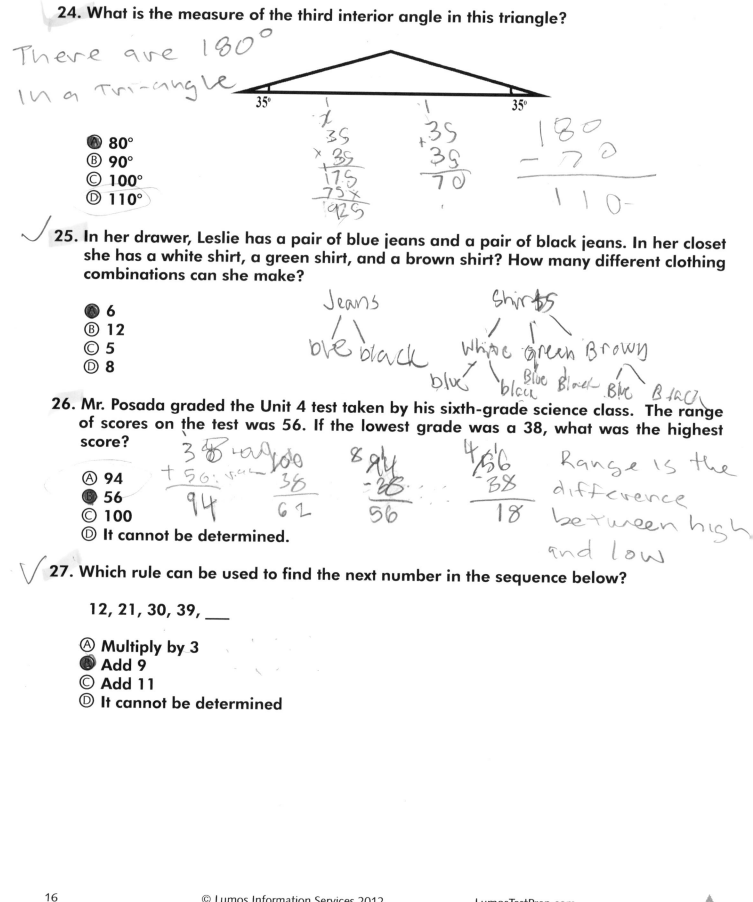

Ⓐ 80°
Ⓑ 90°
Ⓒ 100°
Ⓓ 110°

**25.** In her drawer, Leslie has a pair of blue jeans and a pair of black jeans. In her closet she has a white shirt, a green shirt, and a brown shirt? How many different clothing combinations can she make?

Ⓐ 6
Ⓑ 12
Ⓒ 5
Ⓓ 8

**26.** Mr. Posada graded the Unit 4 test taken by his sixth-grade science class. The range of scores on the test was 56. If the lowest grade was a 38, what was the highest score?

Ⓐ 94
Ⓑ 56
Ⓒ 100
Ⓓ It cannot be determined.

*Range is the difference between high and low*

**27.** Which rule can be used to find the next number in the sequence below?

12, 21, 30, 39, ___

Ⓐ Multiply by 3
Ⓑ Add 9
Ⓒ Add 11
Ⓓ It cannot be determined

LumosTestPrep.com

**Questions 28 and 29 are short constructed response questions.**

- Carefully read each problem before writing your answer.

28. Thomas is cutting a 12-foot long piece of wood into smaller pieces. He makes some pieces that are ½ foot long and some that are ¼ foot long. Assuming he used the whole board, if there were 16 half-foot pieces, how many ¼ foot pieces were there?

29. If the first term in a numerical sequence is 2, and the rule for the sequence is "Add 1.5", what will the sixth term be?

# Extended Constructed Response 2

Here are some reminders for when you are completing this Extended Constructed Response task.

- Carefully read each part of the task before writing your response.
- Be sure to complete all parts of the task.
- Clearly explain your answer and show all your work.
- Your explanation can include words, tables, diagrams, or pictures.
- You may use a calculator and a ruler for this task.

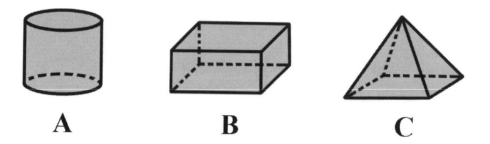

A          B          C

Use the figures above to complete the following:

Use geometric terms to explain how Figures B and C are similar. Note at least two ways.

Use geometric terms to explain how Figures A and B are different. Note at least two ways..

          LumosTestPrep.com

# Work area for Extended Constructed Response 2

# Part C

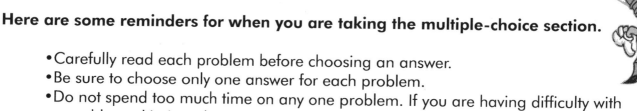

**30.** Find the value of d that makes d – (-5) = 17 a true sentence.

- Ⓐ d = 22
- Ⓑ d = -12
- Ⓒ d = 12
- ⬤ None of these

**31.** The Hoosiers football team gained 20 yards after having lost 8 yards on the previous play. What was their net gain or loss for the two plays?

- Ⓐ They lost 28 yards.
- Ⓑ They gained 12 yards.
- ⬤ They lost 12 yards.
- Ⓓ They gained 28 yards.

**32.** A car gets 16 miles per gallon. How many gallons would the car need to travel 56 miles?

- Ⓐ 2
- Ⓑ 4
- ⬤ 3.5
- Ⓓ 4.5

**33.** What is the prime factoriztion of 30?

- Ⓐ 2 X 15
- Ⓑ 10 X 3
- ⬤ 2 X 3 X 5
- Ⓓ 6 X 5

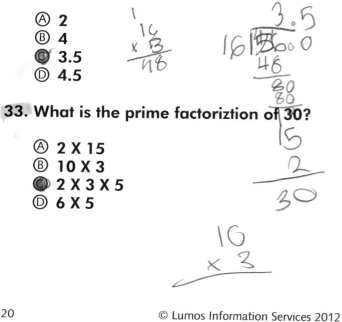

34. If a florist sells 4 dozen roses for $30, how much will 6 dozen roses cost?

Ⓐ $50
Ⓑ $24
Ⓒ $45
Ⓓ $120

35. Which is the proper phrase for this expression?

6 times the sum of a number and 5 is 4 more than twice the number

Ⓐ 6(n + 5) = 2n + 4
Ⓑ 6n + 5 = 2(n+4)
Ⓒ 6n + 5 = 2n + 4
Ⓓ 6(n + 5) = 2n - 4

36. Solve this equation.

n + 86 = 123

Ⓐ n = 37
Ⓑ n = 47
Ⓒ n = 209
Ⓓ n = 219

37. A batting cage offers 8 pitches for a quarter. Raul has $1.50. Which expression could be used to calculate how many pitches Raul could get for his money?

Ⓐ $1.50 x 8
Ⓑ $1.50 ÷ 8
Ⓒ ($1.50 ÷ $0.25) x 8
Ⓓ ($1.50 ÷ $0.25)

38. Look at the number sequence below.

3, 6, 9, 12, ...

Which number sentence could be used to determine the 7th number in the sequence, called n?

Ⓐ n = 12 + 3
Ⓑ n = 12 + 3 + 7
Ⓒ n = 12 + 3 x 3
Ⓓ n = 3 x 12

**39.** James bought 4 lollipops for 15 cents each and 6 candy bars for 45 cents each. Which equation can be used to find the total cost, C, of the lollipops and the candy bars?

Ⓐ C = (4 x $0.45) + (6 x $0.45)
Ⓑ C = (6 x $0.45) + (4 x $0.15)
Ⓒ C = (4 + $0.15) x (6 + $0.45)
Ⓓ C = (4 + 6) x ($0.15 + $0.45)

LumosTestPrep.com

**Questions 40 and 41 are short constructed response questions.**

- Carefully read each problem before writing your answer.

**40. A triangle has a base of 12 and a height of 10. What is the area of the triangle? (in square centimeters)?**

**41. When $\dfrac{5}{16}$ is written as a decimal, what number appears in the thousandths place?**

# Extended Constructed Response 3

Here are some reminders for when you are completing this Extended Constructed Response task.

- Carefully read each part of the task before writing your response.
- Be sure to complete all parts of the task.
- Clearly explain your answer and show all your work.
- Your explanation can include words, tables, diagrams, or pictures.
- You may use a calculator and a ruler for this task.

Wrapping paper rolls are sold in packages of 2, 4, or 6. The following prices apply to the packages:

Package of 2 rolls ------- $1.50
Package of 4 rolls ------- $2.50
Package of 6 rolls ------- $3.50

Lisa needs to buy exactly 12 rolls of wrapping paper for a service project.
How many different combinations of packages can she buy?

Make an organized list of the possibilities.
Of the combinations listed above, which is the least expensive? Show all work and explain your answer.

# Work area for Extended Constructed Response 3

# End Of Diagnostic Test

# Diagnostic Test Answers

## Diagnostic Test Answer Key

### Part A

| Question No. | Answer | Related Lumos Online Workbook | CCSS |
|---|---|---|---|
| 1 | D | Number Lines | 6.NS.6 |
| 2 | C | Area | 6.G.1 |
| 3 | C | Division of Fractions | 6.NS.1 |
| 4 | B | Number Lines | 6.NS.6 |
| 5 | C | Equivalent Ratios and Percentages | 6.RP.3 |
| 6 | B | Area | 6.G.1 |
| 7 | C | Number Theory | 6.NS.4 |
| 8 | B | Division of Fractions | 6.NS.1 |
| 9 | A | Expressions and Variables | 6.EE.2 |
| 10 | B | Division of Whole Numbers | 6.NS.3 |
| 11 | C | Area | 6.G.1 |
| 12 | B | Equivalent Ratios and Percentages | 6.RP.3 |
| 13 | B | Equivalent Expressions I | 6.EE.3 |
| 14 | C | Area | 6.G.1 |
| 15 | B | Solving Inequalities | 6.EE.8 |

## Short Constructed Responses

| | | | |
|---|---|---|---|
| 16 | $2.00 | Division of Whole Numbers | 6.NS.3 |
| 17 | 2 | Nets | 6.G.4 |

# Part B

| Question No. | Answer | Related Lumos Online Workbook | CCSS |
|---|---|---|---|
| 18 | A | Distribution | 6.SP.2 |
| 19 | B | Equivalent Ratios and Percentages | 6.RP.3 |
| 20 | B | Equivalent Expressions I | 6.EE.3 |
| 21 | B | Positive and Negative Numbers | 6.NS.5 |
| 22 | B | Positive and Negative Numbers | 6.NS.5 |
| 23 | D | Coordinate Geometry | 6.G.3 |
| 24 | D | Surface Area and Volume | 6.G.2 |
| 25 | A | Data Interpretation | 6.SP.5 |
| 26 | A | Data Interpretation | 6.SP.5 |
| 27 | B | Expressions and Variables | 6.EE.2 |

## Short Constructed Responses

| Question No. | Answer | Related Lumos Online Workbook | CCSS |
|---|---|---|---|
| 28 | 16 | Division of Fractions | 6.NS.1 |
| 29 | 9.5 | Expressions and Variables | 6.EE.2 |

# Part C

| Question No. | Answer | Related Lumos Online Workbook | CCSS |
|---|---|---|---|
| 30 | C | Expressions and Variables | 6.EE.2 |
| 31 | B | Positive and Negative Numbers | 6.NS.5 |
| 32 | C | Equivalent Ratios and Percentages | 6.RP.3 |
| 33 | C | Number Theory | 6.NS.4 |
| 34 | C | Equivalent Ratios and Percentages | 6.RP.3 |
| 35 | A | Expressions and Variables | 6.EE.2 |
| 36 | A | Solving Equations | 6.EE.7 |
| 37 | C | Solving Equations | 6.EE.7 |
| 38 | C | Equivalent Expressions I | 6.EE.3 |
| 39 | B | Solving Equations | 6.EE.7 |

## Short Constructed Responses

| Question No. | Answer | Related Lumos Online Workbook | CCSS |
|---|---|---|---|
| 40 | 60 cm$^2$ | Area | 6.G.1 |
| 41 | 2 | Division of Whole Numbers | 6.NS.3 |

# Diagnostic Test - Detailed Explanations

## Part A

| Question No. | Answer | Detailed Explanation |
|:---:|:---:|:---|
| 1 | D | The standard form would be written 20.063, since the whole number part is 20 and the decimal part is written .063 (sixtythree thousandths). |
| 2 | C | The third statement is true. By definition, perpendicular lines must cross to form ninety-degree angles, whereas intersecting lines simply need to cross at a point regardless of the angles formed. |
| 3 | C | In order to add fractions with different denominators using the standard procedure, the Least Common Denominator (LCD) must be found. That way only the numerators of the fractions need to be added. |
| 4 | B | As decimals, 3/5 = 0.60 and 3/4 = 0.75. The fraction 5/8 would be found within this range, since 5/8 = 0.625 as a decimal. |
| 5 | C | To find 50% of 65, 65 can be multiplied by 0.5. 65 x 0.5 = 32.5. The answer choice which is the closest approximation of this result is 30. |
| 6 | B | By definition, a quadrilateral must have four sides. Therefore, a triangle is not a quadrilateral since it only has three sides. |
| 7 | C | A prime number is a whole number (greater than 1) which is divisible by only 1 and itself. The set {7, 23, 47} contains three numbers which fit the definition stated above. Each number is divisible by only 1 and itself. |
| 8 | B | The second statement is not true. The multiples of nine would be an infinite set, including such numbers as 9, 18, 27, 36, 45, and so on. |
| 9 | A | Since 3(n + 7) is equal to 33, then (n + 7) must equal 11. (3 x 11 = 33) Therefore, n must equal 4, since 4 + 7 = 11. |
| 10 | B | If each of the 100 workers worked 14 days, the city had to pay for the equivalent of 1,400 days worth of work. 100 x 14 = 1,400. At a rate of $90 per day, that would amount to $126,000. 1,400 x $90 = $126,000. |
| 11 | C | By definition, an obtuse angle measures between 90 and 180 degrees. Therefore, the angle described above (having a measure of about 105 degrees) must be an obtuse angle. |

LumosTestPrep.com

| | | |
|---|---|---|
| 12 | B | To simplify a ratio, first find the Greatest Common Factor (GCF) of the numerator and the denominator. Then, divide each by that number. Here, the GCF is 2. When the numerator and denominator are each divided by 2, the result is 2/11. |
| 13 | B | Each number in this sequence is half of the number preceding it. Therefore, the next two numbers would be 200 (half of 400), and 100 (half of 200). |
| 14 | C | To find the perimeter of the ceiling (a rectangle) the four sides must be totaled. 12 + 16 + 12 + 16 = 56. The perimeter of the ceiling is 56 feet. |
| 15 | B | To solve this inequality, you must add 4 to both sides to isolate the x. Thus, x < 9. |

## Detailed Explanations For SCRs

| | | |
|---|---|---|
| 16 | 100 cubic inches | If each layer of blocks has 20 small blocks, and it takes 5 layers of blocks to fill the large box, then it would take 100 small blocks to fill the large box. Since each small block has a volume of 1 cubic inch, then the volume of the large box must be 100 cubic inches. |
| 17 | 10 | 2   x3   =   x   =   = 10 |

## Part B

| Question No. | Answer | Detailed Explanation |
|---|---|---|
| 18 | A | There is one "F" card and there are two "N" cards. Therefore, the chances of pulling one of these cards is 3 out of 6, or 0.5. |
| 19 | B | To determine if proportions are equivalent, cross multiply the numerator and denominator across the equal sign. Here, 9 * 10 = 90, and 6 * 15 = 90. Therefore, the proportions are equivalent. No other set of proportions allow the products of cross multiplication to be equal. |
| 20 | B | To determine if (3(4x + 1) expression is equivalent, first simplify the expression using the distributive property. 3*4x = 12x; 3*1 = 3. Therefore, the expression is equivalent to 12x+3. |
| 21 | B | It would be most useful for them to know how many bikes each car can carry so that they know how many vehicles will be needed to haul the bikes to the trail. |

| | | |
|---|---|---|
| 22 | B | The size of a window frame would have to be measured with a high degree of accuracy to ensure that the glass fits securely. The other three choices listed do not need as high of a degree of accuracy. |
| 23 | D | A regular polygon must have all equal sides and all equal angles. The last choice (the trapezoid) is not a regular polygon. |
| 24 | D | The sum of the angle measures in a triangle is 180 degrees. The two known angles equal 70 degrees. The third angle in this triangle must measure 180 - 70 = 110 degrees. |
| 25 | A | Leslie has two choices for pants and three choices for shirts. Using the Counting Principle, Leslie can make 2 x 3 = 6 different clothing combinations. |
| 26 | A | The range is the difference between the lowest and the highest numbers in a set. If the lowest grade was a 38, and the range was 56, then the highest score must have been 38 + 56 = 94. |
| 27 | B | Each number in the sequence is 9 more than the number before it. Therefore, the rule for the pattern is "Add 9." |

## Detailed Explanations For SCRs

| | | |
|---|---|---|
| 28 | 16 | If Thomas made 16 half-foot pieces, that would require 8 feet of wood. That would leave 4 feet more. If the remaining 4 feet were cut into 1/4-foot pieces, Thomas could make 16 of them. (Each foot of lumber could be used to make four 1/4-foot pieces.) |
| 29 | 9.5 | The terms in the sequence (up to the sixth term) would be: 2, 3.5, 5, 6.5, 8, 9.5. The equation to solve this problem would be 2 + 1.5 = x, where x represents the sixth number. Since 2 is the first number, and you need five additional sequences to arrive at the sixth number, the equation would become 2 + 5(1.5) = x. Simplified, the equation becomes 2 + 7.5 = x, then x = 9.5. |

## Part C

| Question No. | Answer | Detailed Explanation |
|---|---|---|
| 30 | C | d - (-5) can be rewritten as d + 5. The equation then becomes d + 5 = 17. For this to be true, d must equal 12. |
| 31 | B | A gain of 20 yards could be represented as +20. A loss of 8 yards could be represented as -8. The net for the two plays is +20-8, which equals +12. The Hoosiers gained 12 yards. |

LumosTestPrep.com

| | | |
|---|---|---|
| 32 | C | The correct answer is 3.5. If 1 gallon = 16 miles, 1/16 = x/56. Cross multiply: 16x = 56. Divide each side by 16; x = 3.5. |
| 33 | C | The prime factors of a number are those factors which are prime. 2 X 3 X 5 is the only expression that contains all prime factors; all the rest contain composite factors (factors which can be factored further into their primes) |
| 34 | C | First, set up a proportion for this problem.<br>4/30 x 6/x<br>Then cross multiply: 4*x = 30*6.<br>Simplify: 4x = 180<br>Solve for x by dividing each side by 4.<br>4x/4 = 180/4. x = $45 |
| 35 | A | A is the correct answer: 6(n+5) = 2(n+4). The sum of a "number plus 5" translates to n + 5. 6 times that developes the expression 6(n + 5). "Is" signifies to place an equals sign. Then, "4 more than" means to "add 4" to twice a number, or 2n. Thus, the final expression is 6(n + 5) = 2(n + 4). |
| 36 | A | To solve the equation, 86 can be subtracted from both sides:<br>n + 86 -86 = 123 - 86<br>n = 37 |
| 37 | C | To find how many quarters (or the equivalent of how many quarters) Raul has, you could calculate $1.50 divided by $0.25. Then, that amount of quarters would be multiplied by 8, the number of pitches purchased with each quarter. The final expression would read: ($1.50 ÷ $0.25) x 8 |
| 38 | C | The rule for this sequence is "Add 3." The fourth term is 12. To find the seventh term, 3 would be added to 12 three times. As an equation, this would read: n = 12 + (3 x 3). |
| 39 | B | The cost of the four lollipops would be calculated using 4 x $0.15. The cost of the six candy bars would be calculated using 6 x $0.45. The total cost of all of the items would be the sum of the two expressions written above: C = (6 x $0.45) + (4 x $0.15) |

## Detailed Explanations For SCRs

| | | |
|---|---|---|
| 40 | 60 cm² | The formula for finding a triangle is 1/2bh. Therefore 1/2(12)(10) = 60 cm². |
| 41 | 2 | To express 5/16 as a decimal, you can calculate 5 divided by 16. 5/16 = 0.3125 as a decimal. The thousandths place in this decimal is a 2. |

# Diagnostic Test - Detailed Explanations
## for Extended Constructed Responses

**1: A 3-point response must include the following:**

Allow L to represent the total cost of CD's purchased on-line. The cost for each CD is $10, so n CD's would cost $10(n) when purchased on-line. The company will also add on a shipping fee of $1.50 and a processing fee of $2.50 to the entire order (a total of $4.00 in additional charges). The final equation would be: L = $10(n) + $4.00.

To compare the cost of 8 CD's purchased in each of the two ways:
At the store, C = $13.00(8) = $104.00
On-line, L = $10.00(8) + $4.00 = $84.00
The 8 CD's would cost less if purchased on-line, so that would be the better choice.

**Related Lumos Online Workbook: Solving Equations (CCSS: 6.EE.7)**

**2: A 3-point response must include the following:**

Figures B and C both contain at least one face (flat surface with straight edges).
Figures B and C both contain at least one vertex.
Figure A has two circular bases, whereas Figure B has all rectangular bases.
Figure A has no edges, whereas Figure B has 12 edges.

Note: Other possible comparisons are possible. Geometric terms should always be used in the comparisons.

**Related Lumos Online Workbook: Nets (CCSS: 6.G.4)**

LumosTestPrep.com

**3: A 3-point response must include the following:**

These are the possible combinations of packages that could be bought, and their associated costs:

2, 2, 2, 2, 2, 2 Total cost 6($1.50) = $9.00
2, 2, 2, 2, 4 Total cost 4($1.50) + $2.50 = $8.50
2, 2, 4, 4 Total cost 2($1.50) + 2($2.50) = $8.00
2, 2, 2, 6 Total cost 3($1.50) + $3.50 = $8.00
2, 4, 6 Total cost $1.50 + 2.50 + 3.50 = $7.50
4, 4, 4 Total cost 3($2.50) = $7.50
6, 6 Total cost 2($3.50) = $7.00

Of these combinations, the last one (2 packages of 6) is the least expensive.

**Related Lumos Online Workbook: Data Interpretation (CCSS:6.SP.5)**

# Notes

# Practice Test 1

## Part A

Here are some reminders for when you are taking the multiple-choice section

- Carefully read each problem before choosing an answer.
- Be sure to choose only one answer for each problem.
- Do not circle the correct answer. You must fill the bubble.
- Do not spend too much time on any one problem. If you are having difficulty with a problem, skip it and move on to the next problem.
- You can come back to the skipped problem later if you have time

1. Mr. Donahue spent $37,750 remodeling his kitchen. Of that amount, 1/5 was spent on new appliances. What is the best estimate of the cost of the appliances?

Ⓐ $8,000
Ⓑ $30,000
Ⓒ $15,000
Ⓓ $4,000

2. Diana started at 2 on a number line and moved eight units to the left. She then moved two units to the right. Which integer names the point where she finished after her second move?

Ⓐ -6
Ⓑ 8
Ⓒ -8
Ⓓ -4

3. The unit cost per pint of ice cream is $1.50. At this rate, how much would two gallons of ice cream cost?

Ⓐ $16.00
Ⓑ $24.00
Ⓒ $8.00
Ⓓ $48.00

4. Which of the following statements is not true?

   Ⓐ One hundred thousand is greater than two hundred.
   Ⓑ A quarter million is less than 234,000.
   Ⓒ 524,020 is greater than 524,003.
   Ⓓ A half million is less than three-quarters of a million.

5. The street address of Jack's house is a prime number. Which of the following could be his house number?

   Ⓐ 99
   Ⓑ 87
   Ⓒ 89
   Ⓓ 92

6. Natasha and her coach were practicing for their next softball game. Natasha successfully caught 9 out of 12 balls thrown to her. What percent of the balls thrown to her did she catch?

   Ⓐ 25%
   Ⓑ 75%
   Ⓒ 9%
   Ⓓ 12%

7. Mrs. Paterson earns $36.00 an hour as a manger at a clothing store. At this rate, how much money does she make in an eight and a half hour workday?

   Ⓐ $306.00
   Ⓑ $295.20
   Ⓒ $288.00
   Ⓓ $288.50

8. Juan took a science exam and answered 1/5 of the questions incorrectly. If his exam had 100 questions, how many questions did he answer correctly?

   Ⓐ 100
   Ⓑ 95
   Ⓒ 20
   Ⓓ 80

**9. Which of the following statements is not true?**

Ⓐ $0.66 = \dfrac{2}{3}$

Ⓑ $0.25 = \dfrac{1}{4}$

Ⓒ $0.875 = \dfrac{7}{8}$

Ⓓ $0.45 = \dfrac{9}{20}$

**10. The difference between 5.089 and 4.174 is _____.**

Ⓐ 1.915
Ⓑ 0.915
Ⓒ 1.115
Ⓓ none of these

**11. Which of the following statements best describes these 2 shapes?**

Ⓐ They are similar and congruent.
Ⓑ They are similar, but not congruent.
Ⓒ They are congruent, but not similar.
Ⓓ They are neither similar nor congruent.

**12. What is the missing number in this number pattern?**

729, 243, 81, ___, 9, 3

Ⓐ 13.5
Ⓑ 18
Ⓒ 45
Ⓓ 27

13. Which of the following would best be measured using cubic meters?

    Ⓐ The length of an alligator
    Ⓑ The weight of a large truck
    Ⓒ The area of kitchen
    Ⓓ The volume of a storage container

14. Which of the following objects has a capacity of about 5 gallons?

    Ⓐ A soda can
    Ⓑ A kitchen sink
    Ⓒ A bathtub
    Ⓓ An eye dropper

15. What is the area of a parallelogram with a base of 3 inches and a vertical height of 2 inches?

    Ⓐ 12 square inches
    Ⓑ 3 square inches
    Ⓒ 6 square inches
    Ⓓ 10 square inches

**Questions 16 and 17 are short constructed response questions.**

•Carefully read each problem before writing your answer.

**16. What is the Least Common Multiple (LCM) of the numbers 16 and 40?**

**17. The total cost of three dozen tomato plants is $16.20. What is the price per plant?**

# Extended Constructed Response 1

Here are some reminders for when you are completing this Extended Constructed Response task.

- Carefully read each part of the task before writing your response.
- Be sure to complete all parts of the task.
- Clearly explain your answer and show all your work.
- Your explanation can include words, tables, diagrams, or pictures.
- You may use a calculator and a ruler for this task.

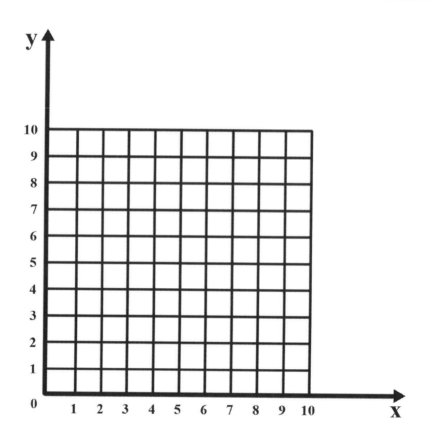

Use the coordinate grid above to complete the following:

Plot and label the following points on the grid:
A: (2, 0) B: (6, 0) C: (6, 4)

Draw a new point, called Point D, on the grid so that figure ABCD is a trapezoid. Draw the trapezoid. The ordered pair naming Point D is _____.

Calculate the area of trapezoid ABCD. Show all work.

LumosTestPrep.com

# Work Area for Extended Constructed Response 1

# Part B

18. **How many lines of symmetry does a regular octagon have?**

    Ⓐ 6
    Ⓑ 8
    Ⓒ 4
    Ⓓ 2

19. **Solve the following inequality:**

    $$\frac{a}{3} < 6$$

    Ⓐ a < 18
    Ⓑ a > 18
    Ⓒ a < 9
    Ⓓ a > 9

20. **Which statement below can be simplified?**

    Ⓐ 3x + 4x + 12x
    Ⓑ 3x + 4y
    Ⓒ 2x - 4xy + 4
    Ⓓ 4y + 2xy

21. **The temperature at noon was 5 degrees F. For the next three hours it dropped at a rate of 2 degrees per hour. Express this change as an integer.**

    Ⓐ + 6 degrees
    Ⓑ + 1 degree
    Ⓒ - 6 degrees
    Ⓓ - 30 degrees

22. Compute the following:

[ - 6 X (2)] X (- 3) =

Ⓐ 12
Ⓑ 36
Ⓒ - 7
Ⓓ 7

23. Which of the following expressions models how the Distributive Property can be used to multiply the following numbers?

6 x 4.31

Ⓐ 6 x 4 + 6 x 0.31
Ⓑ 6 + 4 + 0.31
Ⓒ 6 x 0.31 + 4 x 0.31
Ⓓ 6 x 4 + 0.31

24. During which three-day period did the average temperature drop continually?

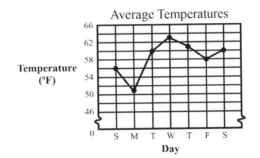

Ⓐ Monday, Tuesday, Wednesday
Ⓑ Tuesday, Wednesday, Thursday
Ⓒ Wednesday, Thursday, Friday
Ⓓ Thursday, Friday, Saturday

**25. Between which two days was there the greatest increase in temperature?**

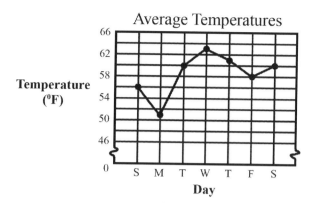

Average Temperatures

Temperature (°F)

Day

Ⓐ Sunday and Monday
Ⓑ Monday and Tuesday
Ⓒ Tuesday and Wednesday
Ⓓ Friday and Saturday

**26. The first five terms in a sequence are written below.**

$$11, 19, 27, 35, 43$$

If the pattern continued, what would the next term be?

Ⓐ 50
Ⓑ 51
Ⓒ 53
Ⓓ 54

**27. If the spinner below is spun 100 times, what section should it land on about 33 times?**

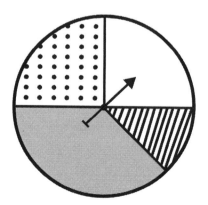

Ⓐ Lined
Ⓑ White
Ⓒ Dotted
Ⓓ Gray

LumosTestPrep.com

**Questions 28 and 29 are short constructed response questions.**

- Carefully read each problem before writing your answer.

**28. Evaluate the following numerical expression:**

$$\frac{[9 + 3(9 - 4)]}{[6(10 - 2)]}$$

**29. 144 inches is equal to how many yards?**

# Extended Constructed Response 2

Here are some reminders for when you are completing this Extended Constructed Response task.

- Carefully read each part of the task before writing your response.
- Be sure to complete all parts of the task.
- Clearly explain your answer and show all your work.
- Your explanation can include words, tables, diagrams, or pictures.
- You may use a calculator and a ruler for this task.

Paris and her brother Antoine are collecting cans for a school recycling project. Each recycled can will earn 4 cents for their school. The goal is for the students to earn $100. So far, Paris has collected 60 cans and Antoine has collected 50 cans. Use the information above to complete the following:

Write two different expressions that could be used to calculate how much money the two children have earned. Explain the meaning behind each of the expressions.

Write an expression that could be used to determine how many cans must be collected altogether in order for the school to meet its goal. Explain your answer.

© Lumos Information Services 2012     LumosTestPrep.com

# Work Area for Extended Constructed Response 2

# Part C

Here are some reminders for when you are taking the multiple-choice section.

- Carefully read each problem before choosing an answer.
- Be sure to choose only one answer for each problem.
- Do not circle the correct answer. You must fill the bubble.
- Do not spend too much time on any one problem. If you are having difficulty with a problem, skip it and move on to the next problem.
- You can come back to the skipped problem later if you have time

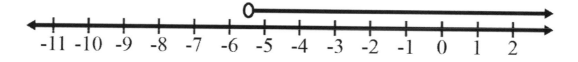

**30. Which inequality is being modeled on the number line above?**

- Ⓐ { x : x > -5.5 }
- Ⓑ { x : x ≥ -5.5 }
- Ⓒ { x : x > -6.5 }
- Ⓓ { x : x ≤ -6.5 }

**31. What is the median of the follow set of numbers?**

28, 23, 32, 25, 23, 22, 20, 34, 27

- Ⓐ 26
- Ⓑ 23
- Ⓒ 25
- Ⓓ 28

LumosTestPrep.com

**32.** Looking at the network below, what is the shortest route starting at point H, going through point R, and ending at point B?

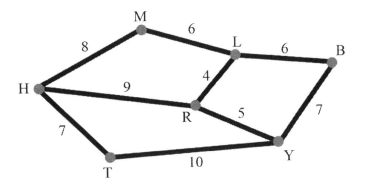

- Ⓐ  HRLB
- Ⓑ  HRYB
- Ⓒ  HMLRYB
- Ⓓ  HMLB

**33.** Solve for x.

2x – 2 = -3x + 23

- Ⓐ  x = 5
- Ⓑ  x = 9
- Ⓒ  x = -5
- Ⓓ  x = 21

**34.** Looking at the double bar graph below, which day of the week had the most ice cream sales?

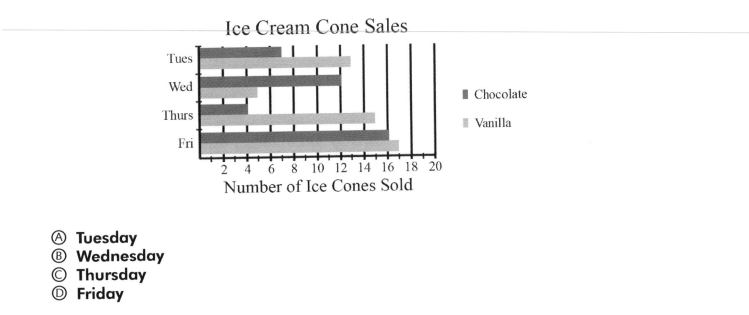

- Ⓐ  **Tuesday**
- Ⓑ  **Wednesday**
- Ⓒ  **Thursday**
- Ⓓ  **Friday**

**35. What is the Greatest Common Factor (GCF) 15 and 40?**

Ⓐ 15
Ⓑ 40
Ⓒ 5
Ⓓ 10

**36. Solve for the variable x:**

$5x - 9 = 9 + 3x$

Ⓐ x = 9
Ⓑ x = -2
Ⓒ x = -9
Ⓓ x = 0

**37. What is the rule of the sequence below?**

34, 30, 22, 10 . . .

Ⓐ The sequence decreases by four.
Ⓑ The sequence decreases by successive factors of four.
Ⓒ The sequence increases by successive multiples of four.
Ⓓ The sequence decreases by successive multiples of four.

**38. Which of these equations has {7} as a solution set?**

Ⓐ n - 10 = 3
Ⓑ n - 4 = 11
Ⓒ n + 6 = 13
Ⓓ 5 + n = -2

**39. Which of the figures below has 4 lines of symmetry and rotational symmetry?**

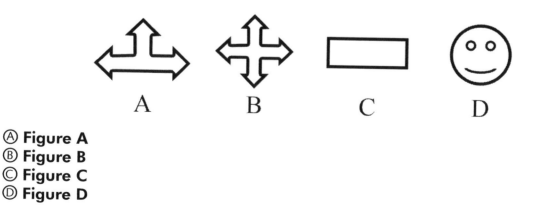

Ⓐ Figure A
Ⓑ Figure B
Ⓒ Figure C
Ⓓ Figure D

Questions 40 and 41 are short constructed response questions.

• Carefully read each problem before writing your answer.

40. A gym teacher is using a rope to enclose a large circular playing field. If the diameter of the playing field is 125 feet, what is its area (rounded to the nearest sq. foot)? Use $\pi = 3.14$

41. What fraction is equivalent to 0.49494949 . . .?

# Extended Constructed Response 3

Here are some reminders for when you are completing this Extended Constructed Response task.

- Carefully read each part of the task before writing your response.
- Be sure to complete all parts of the task.
- Clearly explain your answer and show all your work.
- Your explanation can include words, tables, diagrams, or pictures.
- You may use a calculator and a ruler for this task.

Terri, Kim, Lou, and Steve challenged each other to a race at recess. They are the only four people running in the race. Their friends will watch to see who finishes in first, second, third, and fourth place. Use the information above to complete the following:

Make an organized list showing all of the possible outcomes for the race.

Imagine Lou got tired and had to stop part-way through the race (guaranteeing him a 4th place finish.) How many possible outcomes would there now be? Explain your reasoning.

# Work Area for Extended Constructed Response 3

# End Of Practice Test 1

# Practice Test 1 Answers
## Practice Test 1 Answer Key

## Part A

| Question No. | Answer | Related Lumos Online Workbook | CCSS |
|---|---|---|---|
| 1 | A | Division of Fractions | 6.NS.1 |
| 2 | D | Number Theory | 6.NS.4 |
| 3 | B | Unit Rates | 6.RP.2 |
| 4 | B | Absolute Value | 6.NS.7 |
| 5 | C | Number Theory | 6.NS.4 |
| 6 | B | Equivalent Ratios and Percentages | 6.RP.3 |
| 7 | A | Equivalent Ratios and Percentages | 6.RP.3 |
| 8 | D | Unit Rates | 6.RP.2 |
| 9 | A | Division of Whole Numbers | 6.NS.3 |
| 10 | B | Division of Whole Numbers | 6.NS.3 |
| 11 | D | Coordinate Geometry | 6.G.3 |
| 12 | D | Expressions and Variables | 6.EE.2 |
| 13 | D | Surface Area and Volume | 6.G.2 |
| 14 | B | Surface Area and Volume | 6.G.2 |
| 15 | C | Area | 6.G.1 |

## Short Constructed Responses

| | | | |
|---|---|---|---|
| 16 | 80 | Number Theory | 6.NS.4 |
| 17 | $0.45 | Solving Equations | 6.EE.7 |

## Part B

| Question No. | Answer | Related Lumos Online Workbook | CCSS |
|---|---|---|---|
| 18 | B | Nets | 6.G.4 |
| 19 | A | Expressions and Variables | 6.EE.2 |
| 20 | A | Equivalent Expressions I | 6.EE.3 |
| 21 | C | Positive and Negative Numbers | 6.NS.5 |
| 22 | B | Number Lines | 6.NS.6 |
| 23 | A | Equivalent Expressions I | 6.EE.3 |

LumosTestPrep.com

| 24 | C | Quantitative Relationships | 6.EE.9 |
| 25 | B | Quantitative Relationships | 6.EE.9 |
| 26 | B | Equivalent Expressions I | 6.EE.3 |
| 27 | D | Distribution | 6.SP.2 |

## Short Constructed Responses

| 28 | 1/2 | Absolute Value | 6.NS.7 |
| 29 | 4 | Equivalent Ratios and Percentages | 6.RP.3 |

# Part C

| Question No. | Answer | Related Lumos Online Workbook | CCSS |
|---|---|---|---|
| 30 | A | Solving Inequalities | 6.EE.8 |
| 31 | C | Data Interpretation | 6.SP.5 |
| 32 | A | Coordinate Geometry | 6.G.3 |
| 33 | A | Expressions and Variables | 6.EE.2 |
| 34 | D | Data Interpretation | 6.SP.5 |
| 35 | C | Number Theory | 6.NS.4 |
| 36 | A | Expressions and Variables | 6.EE.2 |
| 37 | D | Absolute Value | 6.NS.7 |
| 38 | C | Expressions and Variables | 6.EE.2 |
| 39 | B | Nets | 6.G.4 |

## Short Constructed Responses

| 40 | 12,266 sq.ft. | Area | 6.G.1 |
| 41 | 49/99 | Division of Whole Numbers | 6.NS.3 |

# Practice Test 1 - Detailed Explanations

## Part A

| Question No. | Answer | Detailed Explanation |
|---|---|---|
| 1 | A | $37,750 is close to $40,000. 1/5 of $40,000 is $8,000. (Divide $40,000 by 5.) Mr. Donahue spent about $8,000 on new appliances. |
| 2 | D | Eight units to the left of 2 would be -6. (2 - 8 = -6) Two units to the right of -6 is -4. (-6 + 2 = -4) Diana ended at -4. |
| 3 | B | One gallon is equal to 8 pints. Therefore, 2 gallons equal 16 pints. At a rate of $1.50 per pint, 16 pints of ice cream would cost $24.00. |
| 4 | B | The second statement is not true. A quarter million is equal to 250,000. That would be greater than 234,000. |
| 5 | C | A prime number is a whole number (greater than 1) that is only divisible by 1 and itself. Of the choices listed, 89 is the only one that fits the definition. (Note: 99 is divisible by 9, 87 is divisible by 3, and 92 is divisible by 2.) |
| 6 | B | 9/12 = 3/4 = 0.75. Natasha caught 75% of the balls thrown to her. |
| 7 | A | To find the amount Mrs. Paterson makes in an eight and a half hour work day, multiply her hourly rate by 8.5. $36.00 x 8.5 = $306.00. She makes $306 in one workday. |
| 8 | D | To find the number of problems Juan answered incorrectly, multiply 1/5 by 100. 1/5 x 100 = 20. Since there were 100 total questions on the exam, Juan must have answered the remaining 80 questions correctly. |
| 9 | A | When written in decimal form, 2/3 is a repeating decimal (0.66666666.....) Therefore, it is not true to say 0.66 = 2/3. |
| 10 | B | If you line up the decimals vertically and subtract (regrouping when necessary) you should find 0.915 to be the difference. |
| 11 | D | "Congruent" means "Same size and same shape." These shapes are not congruent. To be similar, one shape must be an enlarged or reduced version of the other. Angle measurements must still be the same. These shapes are neither congruent nor similar. |
| 12 | D | The rule for this pattern is "Divide by 3" since 729 ÷ 3 = 243 and 243 ÷ 3 = 81. The missing number in the pattern is 27, since 81 ÷ 3 = 27. |
| 13 | D | A cubic meter is a unit of volume, so the fourth choice must be the correct answer. |

LumosTestPrep.com

| 14 | B | Using a one-gallon milk jug as a benchmark, a kitchen sink is probably the closest in capacity to 5 gallons. The other 3 objects are too large or too small. |
| 15 | C | The area of a parallelogram is found by multiplying its base length by its vertical height. The area of this parallelogram is 3 x 2 = 6 in². |

## Detailed Explanations for SCRs

| 16 | 80 | The multiples of 40 are 40, 80, 120, 160, ... Of these, 80 is the first number that is also a multiple of 16 (5 x 16 = 80) Therefore, the LCM of 16 and 40 is 80. |
| 17 | $0.45 | One dozen equals 12. Three dozen equals 36 (3 x 12 = 36). If 36 plants cost a total of $16.20, then let x represent the cost of each plant. Therefore, 36x = $16.20. Divide both sides by 36. Each plant costs $0.45. ($16.20 ÷ 36 = $0.45). |

## Part B

| Question No. | Answer | Detailed Explanation |
| --- | --- | --- |
| 18 | B | The number of lines of symmetry on a regular polygon equals the number of sides it has. Thus, a regular octagon has 8 lines of symmetry. |
| 19 | A | The correct answer is a < 18. To solve this inequality, multiply 3 to each side to isolate the a. This results in a < 18. |
| 20 | A | Only the first expression, 3x + 4x + 12, can be simplified because the term "x" is common to all three. All other choices have different variables. |
| 21 | C | The correct answer is "- 6 degrees". This is because the temperature is dropping negatively two degree each hour, for a total of three hours. - 2 x 3 = - 6. |
| 22 | B | The correct answer is "36". First, simply the terms within the parenthesis: - 6 X 2 = - 12. Then, multiply -12 X -3. Multiplying two negatives results in a positive, so - 12 X - 3 = 36. |
| 23 | A | 4.31 can be decomposed into 4 + 0.31. To multiply 4.31 by 6 would be the same as multiplying each of the two parts above by 6. The Distributive Property allows us to conclude: 6 x 4.31 = (6 x 4) + (6 x 0.31) |
| 24 | C | The line has a downward slope from Wednesday to Thursday and from Thursday to Friday. Therefore, the average temperature continually dropped from Wednesday to Friday. |

| 25 | B | The line has the steepest slope from Monday to Tuesday. Therefore, the greatest increase in average temperature occurred from Monday to Tuesday. |
|---|---|---|
| 26 | B | The rule for this pattern is "Add 8" since 11 + 8 = 19; 19 + 8 = 27; 27 + 8 = 35; and 35 + 8 = 43. The next term would be 43 + 8 = 51. |
| 27 | D | To expect the spinner to land on a color 33 out of 100 times, the color must make up about 1/3 of the spinner. (1/3 = 33 1/3%) The color that makes up about 1/3 of the spinner is Gray. |

## Detailed Explanations for SCRs

| 28 | 1/2 | The numerator of the fraction: 9 + 3(9 - 4) = 9 + 3(5) = 9 + 15 = 24 The denominator of the fraction: 6(10 − 2) = 6(8) = 48. Reducing the fraction: 24/48 = 1/2. |
|---|---|---|
| 29 | 4 | There are 36 inches in a yard. To find the number of yards in 144 inches, you must divide 144 by 36. 144 ÷ 36 = 4. 144 inches = 4 yards. |

## Part C

| Question No. | Answer | Detailed Explanation |
|---|---|---|
| 30 | A | The open circle between -6 and -5 and the arrow pointing to the right indicate that the set will include all numbers greater than -5.5. In set notation, the set is {x : x > -5.5} |
| 31 | C | To find the median of this set, the numbers must first be arranged in increasing order. The set becomes: {20, 22, 23, 23, 25, 27, 28, 32, 34}. The median, or middle number, is 25. |
| 32 | A | The path H - R - L - B has the shortest distance of all paths from H to B, through R. The length of this path is 9 + 4 + 6 = 19. |
| 33 | A | To solve for x, follow the following procedures:<br>2x − 2 = -3x + 23<br>2x +3x -2 = -3x +3x +23 (Add 3x to both sides)<br>5x -2 = 23 (Simplify)<br>5x -2 +2 = 23 + 2 (Add 2 to both sides)<br>5x = 25 (Simplify & Divide both sides by 5)<br>x = 5 (Simplify) |
| 34 | D | Tuesday's total: 7 + 13 = 20<br>Wednesday's total: 12 + 5 = 17<br>Thursday's total: 4 + 15 = 19<br>Friday's total: 16 + 17 = 33<br>Friday's total was the greatest. |

LumosTestPrep.com

| | | |
|---|---|---|
| 35 | C | To find the GCF for a pair of numbers, list the factors for each:<br>15: 1, 3, 5, 15<br>40: 1, 2, 4, 5, 8, 10, 20, 40<br>Then, find the largest valued number that is common to both. Here, the GCF is 5. |
| 36 | A | To solve for x, follow the following procedures:<br>$5x - 9 = 9 + 3x$<br>$5x - 3x - 9 = 9 + 3x - 3x$ (Subtract 3x from both sides)<br>$2x - 9 = 9$ (Simplify)<br>$2x - 9 + 9 = 9 + 9$ (Add 9 to both sides)<br>$2x = 18$ (Simplify & Divide both sides by 2)<br>$x = 9$ (Simplify) |
| 37 | D | The difference between 34 and 30 is 4. The difference between 30 and 22 is 8. The difference between 22 and 10 is 12. The rule is to subtract successive multiples of 4 (4, 8, 12, etc.) |
| 38 | C | $n + 6 = 13$ has {7} as a solution set since $7 + 6 = 13$. |
| 39 | B | The second figure (Figure B) has 4 lines of symmetry (one vertical, one horizontal, and two diagonal) and rotational symmetry (90 degrees). |

## Detailed Explanations for SCRs

| | | |
|---|---|---|
| 40 | 12,266 sq.ft. | The area of a circle can be found using: $A = \pi \times r^2$<br>The radius of a circle is half of its diameter. The radius of this circle is $125/2 = 62.5$ feet. Using the formula: $A = (3.14) \times (62.5)^2 = 12,266$ ft$^2$ (rounded to the nearest sq. foot). |
| 41 | 49/99 | Follow this procedure to convert the decimal to a fraction:<br>Let $x = 0.494949494949.....$<br>Then $100x = 49.49494949......$<br>Subtract the first equation from the second equation.<br>$99x = 49$<br>$x = 49/99$ |

# Practice Test 1 - Detailed Explanations
## for Extended Constructed Responses

**1: A 3-point response must include the following:**

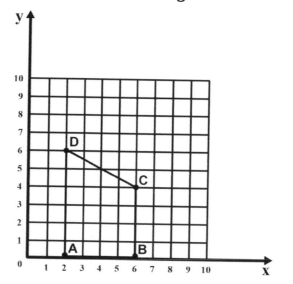

The graph above shows one of many possible solutions. Point D was plotted at (2,6), thus forming a trapezoid. Figure ABCD is a trapezoid because it is a closed figure with four sides, and one pair of sides is parallel. (Side AD is parallel to side BC.)

To calculate the area of the trapezoid, used the formula: A = (1/2)(h)(b1 + b2), where h is the perpendicular height of the trapezoid, and b1 and b2 are the lengths of the parallel bases. In trapezoid ABCD, b1 = AD = 6, b2 = BC = 4, and h = AB = 4. Substituting into the formula: A = (1/2)(4)(6 + 4) = 20 square units.

**Related Lumos Online Workbook: Coordinate Geometry (CCSS:6.G.3)**

**2: A 3-point response must include the following:**

One possible method for totaling the amount of money earned is to figure out the amount each child has earned and then add the two values together.

Paris has collected 60 cans. At a rate of $0.04 each, she has earned 60($0.04). Antoine has collected 50 cans. At the same rate, he has earned 50($0.04) Together, they have earned 60($0.04) + 50($0.04)

Another possible way of figuring out their total is to add the cans they have collected, and then multiply the amount by the monetary rate. Together, they have collected 60 + 50 = 110 cans. At a rate of $0.04 per can, they have raised 110($0.04).

If each can collected is worth $0.04 to the school, then the children need to collect an amount of cans equal to $100.00 divided by $0.04, or 100/0.04 cans.

**Related Lumos Online Workbook: Quantitative Relationships (CCSS: 6.EE.9)**

LumosTestPrep.com

### 3: A 3-point response must include the following:

The four runners are Terri (T), Kim (K), Lou (L), and Steve (S).

There are 24 possible outcomes for the race. Here they are (each one listed from 1st place to 4th place finish):

TKLS TKSL TSKL TSLK TLKS TLSK
KTLS KTSL KLST KLTS KSLT KSTL
LKST LKTS LSKT LSTK LTKS LTSK
STKL STLK SKLT SKTL SLTK SLKT

If Lou were to be guaranteed a 4th place finish, then the only possibilities left in the list above would be those with L in the fourth position:

TKSL TSKL KTSL KSTL STKL SKTL

There are a total of 6 possibilities.

**Related Lumos Online Workbook: Data Interpretation (CCSS: 6.SP.5)**

# Notes

  LumosTestPrep.com

# Practice Test 2

Student Name: _____

Test Date: _____

Start Time: _____

End Time: _____

## Part A

Here are some reminders for when you are taking the multiple-choice section.

- Carefully read each problem before choosing an answer.
- Be sure to choose only one answer for each problem.
- Do not circle the correct answer. You must fill the bubble.
- Do not spend too much time on any one problem. If you are having difficulty with a problem, skip it and move on to the next problem.
- You can come back to the skipped problem later if you have time

1. Nick worked 14 hours one week and 20 hours the following week at the same store. He earned a total of $289. How much did he earn per hour?

   Ⓐ $8.50
   Ⓑ $16.00
   Ⓒ $7.50
   Ⓓ $8.00

2. Which of these is the standard form of two and sixty-three ten-thousandths?

   Ⓐ 2.63000
   Ⓑ 263.0001
   Ⓒ 2.0063
   Ⓓ 2.00063

3. After making withdrawals of $12.55 and $26.45, you have a balance of $175.90 in your savings account. What was the balance in your account before these two withdrawals were made?

   Ⓐ $215.00
   Ⓑ $214.90
   Ⓒ $136.90
   Ⓓ It cannot be determined.

4. Estimate the sum of $21\frac{1}{4} + 25\frac{1}{2}$

    Ⓐ 45
    Ⓑ 47
    Ⓒ 32
    Ⓓ 40

5. If Arthur collects a total of $48 every two weeks, what is the closest estimate to the number of weeks it will take him to collect $299.50 for a new video game system?

    Ⓐ 5
    Ⓑ 6
    Ⓒ 12
    Ⓓ 16

6. The value of a number rounded to the nearest ten is 4,590. Which of the following integers could be that number?

    Ⓐ 4,581
    Ⓑ 4,585
    Ⓒ 4,692
    Ⓓ 4,595

7. A string measures 8.7 cm in length. It is cut into three equal pieces. Each piece is _____ long.

    Ⓐ between 2.5 and 3.0 cm
    Ⓑ less than 2.5 cm
    Ⓒ between 3.0 and 3.2 cm
    Ⓓ greater than 3.2 cm

8. Find the value of the expression below.

$$3 + 2 (8 - 2) \div 3$$

    Ⓐ 5
    Ⓑ 7
    Ⓒ 10
    Ⓓ 15

LumosTestPrep.com

**9. Which type of transformation is shown below?**

Ⓐ Reflection
Ⓑ Rotation
Ⓒ Translation
Ⓓ Expansion

**10. Which of the following nets below can be folded to form a square pyramid?**

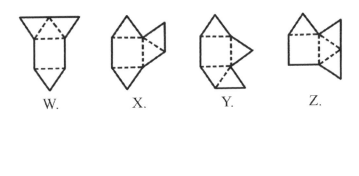

W.    X.    Y.    Z.

Ⓐ W
Ⓑ X
Ⓒ Y
Ⓓ Z

**11. In the triangle below, angles A and C together measure 82 degrees. What is the measure of angle B?**

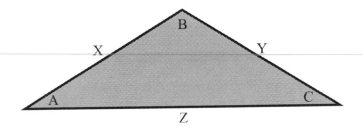

Ⓐ 98 degrees
Ⓑ 108 degrees
Ⓒ 112 degrees
Ⓓ 82 degrees

**12. In the figure below, which two shapes appear to be congruent?**

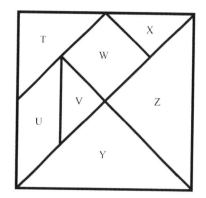

Ⓐ V and W
Ⓑ U and W
Ⓒ T and X
Ⓓ Z and Y

**13. Express the inequality represented on the number line.**

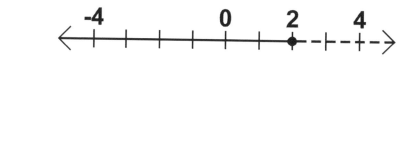

Ⓐ x ≤ 2
Ⓑ x ≥ 2
Ⓒ x < 2
Ⓓ x > 2

**14. If Angle A has a greater measure than Angle B, which of these is a possible measure for Angle A?**

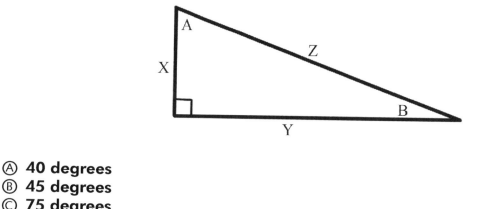

Ⓐ 40 degrees
Ⓑ 45 degrees
Ⓒ 75 degrees
Ⓓ 90 degrees

## 15. How many edges does this solid figure have?

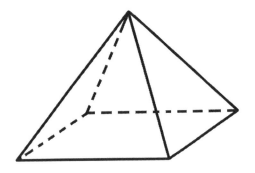

- Ⓐ 5
- Ⓑ 6
- Ⓒ 8
- Ⓓ 9

**Questions 16 and 17 are short constructed response questions.**

• Carefully read each problem before writing your answer.

16. One thousand middle school students participated in an online survey. The students were asked to name their favorite vacation spot. 1/20 of the students chose Florida. How many students chose a spot other than Florida?

17. Three number cubes (dice) are rolled. What is the probability that a "6" is rolled on all three of the number cubes? Express the probability as a fraction in lowest terms.

LumosTestPrep.com

# Extended Constructed Response 1

Here are some reminders for when you are completing this Extended Constructed Response task.

- Carefully read each part of the task before writing your response.
- Be sure to complete all parts of the task.
- Clearly explain your answer and show all your work.
- Your explanation can include words, tables, diagrams, or pictures.
- You may use a calculator and a ruler for this task.

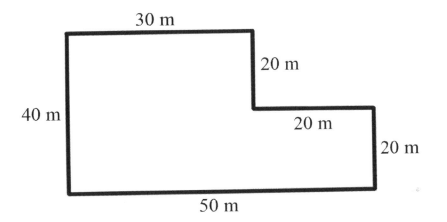

Find two different ways to calculate the area of the figure shown above. Be sure to show your work for each of the calculations.

# Work Area for Extended Constructed Response 1

LumosTestPrep.com

# Part B

Here are some reminders for when you are taking the multiple-choice section.

- Carefully read each problem before choosing an answer.
- Be sure to choose only one answer for each problem.
- Do not circle the correct answer. You must fill the bubble.
- Do not spend too much time on any one problem. If you are having difficulty with a problem, skip it and move on to the next problem.
- You can come back to the skipped problem later if you have time

18. Jasper was practicing soccer in his backyard. He attempted 125 shots on the goal. If 40% of the attempts were misses and the rest were goals, how many of the attempts were goals?

Ⓐ 50
Ⓑ 60
Ⓒ 75
Ⓓ none of these

19. A school auditorium has 650 seats. The seats are arranged in 26 equal rows. How many seats are in each row?

Ⓐ 20
Ⓑ 25
Ⓒ 32
Ⓓ 250

20. Complete the conversion:

4.5 tons = _____ lb

Ⓐ 9,000
Ⓑ 4,500
Ⓒ 900
Ⓓ 450

**21. Evaluate 3(x - 2) - 12/x + 5 for x = 2**

(A) 1
(B) -1
(C) 4
(D) -5

**22. Describe the correlation exhibited in this graph.**

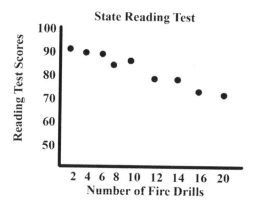

(A) **A positive correlation**
(B) **A negative correlation**
(C) **No correlation**
(D) **It cannot be determined**

**23. Morgan wanted to list the prime numbers less than twenty. Which prime number is missing from her list?**

2, 3, 7, 11, 13, 17, 19

(A) 1
(B) 5
(C) 9
(D) 15

**24. Which of these statements is true?**

(A) 5,028 = (5 x 1,000) + (2 x 100) + ( 8 x 10)
(B) 5,208 = (5 x 1,000) + (2 x 100) + (8 x 10)
(C) 528 = (5 x 100) + (2 x 10) + (8 x 1)
(D) 5,280 = (5 x 100) + (2 x 10) + (8 x 1)

LumosTestPrep.com

25. Peter is trying to save money to buy a laptop computer. He earns an allowance of $10.00 per week from his parents. He also cuts lawns for his neighbors. He earns $8.00 for each lawn he cuts. Using c to represent the number of lawns Peter cuts, which expression could be used to calculate the money Peter makes during a given week?

Ⓐ $10.00 + c
Ⓑ $10.00(c) + $8.00
Ⓒ $10.00 + $8.00(c)
Ⓓ ($18.00)(c)

26. Which of the following situations would most likely involve an increasing trend?

Ⓐ The speed of a ball flying through the air
Ⓑ The amount of water left in a puddle on a sunny day
Ⓒ The height of a child during his years in school
Ⓓ The altitude of a plane during its approach to an airport

27. Which of the following expressions simplifies to a whole number?

Ⓐ [6 + 4(9)] / [6(6) + 2]
Ⓑ [11(4) – 2(2)] / [3 + 2(2)]
Ⓒ [(7 + 1) x 4] / [2(2)]
Ⓓ none of these

**Questions 28 and 29 are short constructed response questions.**

• Carefully read each problem before writing your answer.

**28. What is the greatest number of right angles that a trapezoid can have?**

**29. How many perfect squares are found between 0 and 200?**

LumosTestPrep.com

# Extended Constructed Response 2

Here are some reminders for when you are completing this Extended Constructed Response task.

- Carefully read each part of the task before writing your response.
- Be sure to complete all parts of the task.
- Clearly explain your answer and show all your work.
- Your explanation can include words, tables, diagrams, or pictures.
- You may use a calculator and a ruler for this task.

Oliver wants to hire a landscaper to plant some trees and flowers around his large concrete patio. Green Thumb Landscaping charges a flat rate of $200 for a design layout, plus labor costs of $50.00 per hour. Spruce-Up Landscaping charges $350 for a design layout, plus $35.00 per hour labor costs.

**Use the information above to complete the following:**
Let n represent the number of hours needed to complete the landscaping job. Write an equation that can be used to find the total cost of the job if it is done by Green Thumb Landscaping.

Write an equation that can be used to find the total cost for Spruce-Up Landscaping. Compare the total cost of each company if the job will take approximately 8 hours to complete. Show all work.

# Work Area for Extended Constructed Response 2

# Part C

Here are some reminders for when you are taking the multiple-choice section.

- Carefully read each problem before choosing an answer.
- Be sure to choose only one answer for each problem.
- Do not circle the correct answer. You must fill the bubble.
- Do not spend too much time on any one problem. If you are having difficulty with a problem, skip it and move on to the next problem.
- You can come back to the skipped problem later if you have time

30. Write the following expression: 25% of some number subtracted from seven hundred

  Ⓐ 700 - .25y
  Ⓑ 700*25 - y
  Ⓒ 25y - 700
  Ⓓ .25 - 700

31. Find the equivalent expression for 5(9x - 7)

  Ⓐ 4x - 2
  Ⓑ 14x - 12
  Ⓒ 45x - 35
  Ⓓ 45x + 35

32. Find the area of a rectangle whose length is 24 yards and width is 17 yards.

  Ⓐ 41 yd²
  Ⓑ 408 yd²
  Ⓒ 204 yd²
  Ⓓ 7 yd²

33. Solve for x in the following equation:

$$x - 16 = 32$$

  Ⓐ x = 16
  Ⓑ x = 48
  Ⓒ x = 44
  Ⓓ x = -16

34. Which of the following computations will always yield a positive result?

    (A) Adding a positive integer to a negative integer
    (B) Adding two negative integers
    (C) Multiplying two negative integers
    (D) Multiplying a negative integer by zero

35. If the rule for the following pattern is "Divide by 2," which of the following numbers will not be part of the sequence?

    200, 100, 50, . . .

    (A) 25
    (B) 12.5
    (C) 0
    (D) 6.25

36. A right triangle has legs lengths of 16 and 30. Use the Pythagorean Theorem to find the length of the hypotenuse.

    (A) c = 34
    (B) c = 1,156
    (C) c = 46
    (D) c = 14

37. A classroom has 15 boys and 10 girls. What is the simplified ratio of boys to girls?

    (A) 10:15
    (B) 15:10
    (C) 3/2
    (D) 2/3

38. Nina had a 30 foot by 20 foot backyard that she wanted to enclose with a fence. How many feet of fencing would it take to enclose the yard?

    (A) 10 feet
    (B) 100 feet
    (C) 50 feet
    (D) 25 feet

    

**39. Adeline and Connie are collecting cards. What is the ratio of Adeline's cards to Connie's cards?**

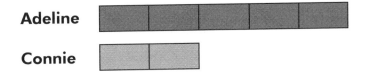

Adeline

Connie

Ⓐ 2/5
Ⓑ 5/2
Ⓒ 3
Ⓓ -3

**Questions 40 and 41 are short constructed response questions.**

• Carefully read each problem before writing your answer.

40. Trevor has a ten-dollar bill. He goes to the stationary store to buy pencils and notebooks. Pencils cost 25 cents each and notebooks cost $2.00 each. If he buys a dozen pencils, how many notebooks can he buy? (Assume there is no tax.)

41. A storage container is 8 feet tall. The base of the container is a rectangle with area 144 square feet. What is the volume of the container? (in cubic feet)

© Lumos Information Services 2012     LumosTestPrep.com

# Extended Constructed Response 3

Here are some reminders for when you are completing this Extended Constructed Response task.

- Carefully read each part of the task before writing your response.
- Be sure to complete all parts of the task.
- Clearly explain your answer and show all your work.
- Your explanation can include words, tables, diagrams, or pictures.
- You may use a calculator and a ruler for this task.

Use the following set of numbers to complete this exercise:

{12, 15, 18, 12, 15, 18, 6, 24, 33}

Calculate the mean of the set. Show your work.

Calculate the median of the set. Show your work.

Add one number to the set so that the mean changes, but the median stays the same. Show your work and explain you answer.

# Work Area for Extended Constructed Response 3

# End Of Practice Test 2

# Practice Test 2 Answers
## Practice Test 2 Answer Key

## Part A

| Question No. | Answer | Related Lumos Online Workbook | CCSS |
|---|---|---|---|
| 1 | A | Division of Whole Numbers | 6.NS.3 |
| 2 | C | Absolute Value | 6.NS.7 |
| 3 | B | Positive and Negative Numbers | 6.NS.5 |
| 4 | B | Division of Fractions | 6.NS.1 |
| 5 | C | Division of Whole Numbers | 6.NS.3 |
| 6 | B | Absolute Value | 6.NS.7 |
| 7 | A | Division of Fractions | 6.NS.1 |
| 8 | B | Equivalent Expressions I | 6.EE.3 |
| 9 | A | Nets | 6.G.4 |
| 10 | A | Nets | 6.G.4 |
| 11 | A | Area | 6.G.1 |
| 12 | D | Coordinate Geometry | 6.G.3 |
| 13 | B | Solving Inequalities | 6.EE.8 |
| 14 | C | Area | 6.G.1 |
| 15 | C | Coordinate Geometry | 6.G.3 |

## Short Constructed Responses

| | | | |
|---|---|---|---|
| 16 | 950 | Equivalent Ratios and Percentages | 6.RP.3 |
| 17 | 1/216 | Data Interpretation | 6.SP.5 |

## Part B

| Question No. | Answer | Related Lumos Online Workbook | CCSS |
|---|---|---|---|
| 18 | C | Equivalent Ratios and Percentages | 6.RP.3 |
| 19 | B | Operations | 6.NS.2 |
| 20 | A | Unit Rates | 6.RP.2 |
| 21 | B | Expressions and Variables | 6.EE.2 |
| 22 | B | Data Interpretation | 6.SP.5 |

| | | | |
|---|---|---|---|
| 23 | B | Number Theory | 6.NS.4 |
| 24 | C | Operations | 6.NS.2 |
| 25 | C | Writing Expressions | 6.EE.6 |
| 26 | C | Data Interpretation | 6.SP.5 |
| 27 | C | Expressions and Variables | 6.EE.2 |

## Short Constructed Responses

| | | | |
|---|---|---|---|
| 28 | 2 | Surface Area and Volume | 6.G.2 |
| 29 | 14 | Division of Whole Numbers | 6.NS.3 |

# Part C

| Question No. | Answer | Related Lumos Online Workbook | CCSS |
|---|---|---|---|
| 30 | A | Equivalent Expressions I | 6.EE.3 |
| 31 | C | Equivalent Expressions I | 6.EE.3 |
| 32 | B | Expressions and Variables | 6.EE.2 |
| 33 | B | Expressions and Variables | 6.EE.2 |
| 34 | C | Absolute Value | 6.NS.7 |
| 35 | C | Whole Number Exponents | 6.EE.1 |
| 36 | A | Equivalent Expressions I | 6.EE.3 |
| 37 | C | Expressing Ratios | 6.RP.1 |
| 38 | B | Equivalent Expressions I | 6.EE.3 |
| 39 | B | Equivalent Ratios and Percentages | 6.RP.3 |

## Short Constructed Responses

| | | | |
|---|---|---|---|
| 40 | 3 | Operations | 6.NS.2 |
| 41 | 1,152 cu. ft. | Surface Area and Volume | 6.G.2 |

LumosTestPrep.com

# Practice Test 2 - Detailed Explanations

## Part A

| Question No. | Answer | Detailed Explanation |
|---|---|---|
| 1 | A | Altogether, Nick worked 34 hours during the two-week period. If his total earnings were $289, then to find his hourly rate you can divide the total earnings by the number of hours worked. $289 divided by 34 equals $8.50. Nick earned $8.50 per hour. |
| 2 | C | The whole number part of this number is 2. The fractional (decimal) part is 0.0063 (sixty-three ten-thousandths). Therefore, 2.0063 would be the standard form of this number. |
| 3 | B | Because withdrawals involve taking money out of the account, to find the balance at the beginning, the money withdrawn would have to be added back into the account balance. The ending balance was $175.90. Adding the two withdrawals back into the account, $175.90 + 12.55 + 26.45 = $214.90. The original account balance was $214.90. |
| 4 | B | To estimate the sum, break the mixed numbers into their whole number and fractional parts. The sum can be rewritten: (21 + 25) + (1/4 + 1/2). 21 + 25 = 46. 1/4 + 1/2 equals about 1 whole. So, the estimated sum is about 46 + 1 = 47. |
| 5 | C | $48 is close to $50. $299.50 is around $300. So, Arthur will need 6 two-week periods to earn enough money to buy the game system ($300 / $50 = 6). Six two-week periods are the same as 12 weeks. |
| 6 | B | The integers that round to 4,590 when rounded to the nearest ten are 4,585 through 4,594. The answer choice found in that range is 4,585. |
| 7 | A | 8.7 cm divided by 3 equals 2.9 cm. Each piece of string is 2.9 cm long. That falls in the range from 2.5 cm to 3.0 cm. |
| 8 | B | Using the Order of Operations, (8 - 2) would be done first. Then multiplication and division would be done from left to right in the expression. Finally, addition would be done. 3 + 2 (8 - 2) ÷ 3 = 3 + 2(6) ÷ 3 = 3 + 12 ÷ 3 = 3 + 4 = 7. |
| 9 | A | The second figure is a mirror image of the first. Therefore a flip, or a reflection, has been done. |
| 10 | A | The first net would fold up to make a square pyramid. Each of the other nets would result in an overlapping of one or more of the faces. |

| | | |
|---|---|---|
| 11 | A | The measures of the angles in a triangle total 180 degrees. If Angles A and C measure 82 degrees together, then the measure of Angle B is 180 - 82 = 98 degrees. |
| 12 | D | Congruent figures must be the same size and the same shape. In this figure, shapes Z and Y appear to be the same size and the same shape. Therefore, Z and Y are congruent. |
| 13 | B | A closed circle on a number line represents "equal to". The dashed line is pointing in the positive, or "greater than" direction. Therefore, the inequality should read x ≥ 2 |
| 14 | C | Since the sum of the angle measures in a triangle must be 180 degrees, and this triangle has a right angle (90 degree angle), Angles A and B must total 90 degrees. Angle A could not measure 45 degrees, because Angle B would also have to equal 45 degrees, and we are told they are not the same. Angle A could not measure 90 degrees, because Angle B would then measure 0, which is impossible. Angle A could not measure 40 degrees, because Angle B measures less than Angle A, and the sum of the measures of Angles A and B would be too low. The only possible answer of the four given is 75 degrees. |
| 15 | C | The edges are the line segments where faces meet on a solid figure. This figure has 8 edges. |

## Detailed Explanations for SCRs

| | | |
|---|---|---|
| 16 | 950 | 1/20 of 1,000 is 50. (1/20 x 1,000 = 50). Thus, 50 students chose Florida as their favorite vacation spot. That leaves 950 students who chose a spot other than Florida. 1,000 - 50 = 950 |
| 17 | 1/216 | The probability of a 6 being rolled on all three of the dice is the product of the probabilities of it happening on each die separately. Each die has a 1/6 chance of coming up a 6 when rolled. The probability of it happening on all three dice is (1/6) x (1/6) x (1/6) = 1/216 |

## Part B

| Question No. | Answer | Detailed Explanation |
|---|---|---|
| 18 | C | If Jasper missed 40% of the time, then he made a goal 60% of the time. (The percents must add to 100%). 60% of 125 = 0.60 x 125 = 75. He made 75 goals. |
| 19 | B | Because the rows are all equal, we can use division to find the number of seats in each row. 650 ÷ 26 = 25. There are 25 seats in each row. |

LumosTestPrep.com

| 20 | A | 1 Ton = 2,000 pounds. To change 4.5 Tons to pounds: 4.5 T x (2,000 lb / 1 T) = 9,000 lb. |
|----|---|---|
| 21 | B | The correct answer is -1. First, substitute the value for x. 3[(2) - 2] - 12/2 + 5. Use the order of operations to simplify, starting with the parenthesis: 3(0) - 12/2 + 5<br>Multiply and divide, from left to right: 0 - 6 + 5.<br>Add and subtract from left to right: -1 |
| 22 | B | As the number of fire drills (the independent variable) increases, the reading scores (the dependent variable) decrease. Therefore, this graph shows a negative correlation. |
| 23 | B | A prime number is a whole number (greater than 1) which is divisible only by 1 and itself. Morgan has left the number 5 out of her list. 5 is also a prime number less than 20. |
| 24 | C | The third statement is true. 528 = 5 hundreds, 2 tens, and 8 ones = (5 x 100) + (2 x 10) + (8 x 1). |
| 25 | C | To find the amount of money Peter makes cutting lawns, multiply the number of lawns he cuts, c, by $8.00. He earns $8.00(c). His allowance of $10.00 is a flat rate. Therefore, in a given week he earns $10.00 + $8.00(c). |
| 26 | C | A child grows during his/her school years, so the height of the child throughout the school years should show an increasing trend. |
| 27 | C | The first expression simplifies to 42/38, which is not a whole number. The second expression simplifies to 40/7, which is also not a whole number. The third expression simplifies to 32/4, which is a whole number (8). |

## Detailed Explanations for SCRs

| 28 | 2 | The sum of the angle measures in a trapezoid is 360 degrees. A trapezoid can have 2 right angles. The shape is called a right trapezoid. It cannot have more than two right angles, because then it would become a rectangle. By definition, a rectangle is not a trapezoid, since it has two pairs of parallel sides, not just one pair. |
|----|---|---|
| 29 | 14 | The smallest perfect square in this range is 1 (1 x 1 = 1). The greatest perfect square in this range is 196 (14 x 14 = 196). Therefore, there are 14 perfect squares between 0 and 200. |

| Question No. | Answer | Detailed Explanation |
|---|---|---|
| 30 | A | 25% of a number can be expressed numerically as .25; "subtracted from" means to take away from a preceding term; therefore: 700 - .25y |
| 31 | C | The correct answer is 45x - 35. Distribute the factor of 5 to each item inside the parenthesis: 5*9x - 5*7. Simplify: 45x - 35. |
| 32 | B | The formula for finding area is a = LW. Let L = 24 and W = 17. Substitute: a = (24)(17) Simplify a = 408 yd2 Note that area is always expressed in units "squared" |
| 33 | B | To solve for x in x - 16 = 32, add 16 to both sides of the equation. x - 16 + 16 = 32 + 16 x = 48 |
| 34 | C | The product of two negative numbers is always a positive number. Therefore, the third choice is correct. |
| 35 | C | Zero will never appear in this sequence. You can divide a number by 2 continually and never arrive at zero. The result will always be a positive number. The other three numbers, 25, 12.5, and 6.25, would be found in this sequence. |
| 36 | A | The Pythagorean Theorem can be expressed as $c^2 = a^2 + b^2$, where the legs are represented by a and b, and the hypotenuse is represented by c. Substitute the values given from the problem: $c^2 = (16)^2 + (30)^2$, Then, simplify using the Order of Operations, starting with the parenthesis: $c^2 = 256 + 900$ $c^2 = 1,156$ The square root of c is equal to the length of the hypotenuse. So find the square root of 1,156. This makes c = 34. |
| 37 | C | A ratio compares two quantities. If there are 15 boys and 10 girls, the ratio can be expressed as 15:10, but when simplified, can be expressed as 3/2 |
| 38 | B | The formula for perimeter is 2(L + W). Here, let L = 20 and W = 30: 2(20 + 30). Then, simplify using the order of operations, starting with the parenthesis: 2(50). Next, use multiplication to simplify: 100. |
| 39 | B | Ratio is expressed as a part to a part. Here, Adelines "part" is 5, and Connie's "part" is 2. Therefore, the correct ratio is 5:2. |

# Detailed Explanations for SCRs

| | | |
|---|---|---|
| 40 | 3 | A dozen (12) pencils would cost $0.25 x 12 = $3.00. That would leave Trevor $7.00 to buy notebooks. He could buy 3 notebooks with that amount of money. |
| 41 | 1,152 cu. ft. | The volume of the rectangular storage container can be found by multiplying its base area by its height. 144 x 8 = 1,152 cubic feet. |

# Practice Test 2 - Detailed Explanations
## for Extended Constructed Responses

**1:  A 3-point response must include the following:**

One possible method for calculating the area of the figure is to separate it into two smaller figures. The figure can be separated into two rectangles: one measuring 20 m by 30 m, and the other measuring 20 m by 50 m. The area of each of these rectangles is 20 x 30 = 600 sq. m, and 20 x 50 = 1,000 sq. m. In all, the area of the entire figure is 600 + 1,000 = 1,600 square meters.

Another method is to find the area of a larger rectangle which contains the figure and then to subtract the area not part of the figure. This figure is contained within a rectangle measuring 40 m by 50 m. The area of this rectangle is 40 x 50 = 2,000 sq. m. The area of that rectangle that is not part of the figure is a smaller rectangle measuring 20 m by 20 m (or 400 sq. m.) Thus, the area of the figure is 2,000 − 400 = 1,600 square meters.

**Related Lumos Online Workbook: Area (CCSS: 6.G.1)**

**2:  A 3-point response must include the following:**

If Green Thumb Landscapers were to do the job, they would charge $200 plus $50(n) for the n hours of labor costs. In equation form, the cost (G) of using Green Thumb is: G = $200 + $50(n)

If Spruce-Up Landscapers were to do the job, they would charge $350 plus $35(n) for n hours of labor costs. In equation form, the cost (S) of using Spruce-Up is: S = $350 + $35(n)

If the job were to take 8 hours, the cost of using each landscaper would be:
G = $200 + $50(8) = $600 for Green Thumb
S = $350 + $35(8) = $630 for Spruce-Up

If the job were to take 8 hours, Green Thumb Landscapers would be $30 cheaper than Spruce-Up Landscapers.

**Related Lumos Online Workbook: Quantitative Relationships (CCSS: 6.EE.9)**

LumosTestPrep.com

**3:  A 3-point response must include the following:**

To find the mean of this set of 9 numbers, add the numbers together then divide by 9.

12 + 15 + 18 + 12 + 15 + 18 + 6 + 24 + 33 = 153

153/9 = 17. The mean is 17.

To find the median value, list the numbers in order from least to greatest, then locate the middle value.

The new set becomes: {6, 12, 12, 15, 15, 18, 18, 24, 33}. The median value is 15.

In order to add one more number to the set without changing the median, the number must be less than or equal to 15. A number greater than 15 would cause the median to increase. A number less than or equal to 15 would not change the median since the fifth and sixth terms in the new set would both be 15, resulting in a median of 15. Because the mean of the original set was greater than 15, the mean will change if a number less than or equal to 15 was added to the set. The mean would only stay the same if a value equal to the original mean (17) was added to the set. Any number less than or equal to 15 would be an acceptable answer to this exercise.

**Related Lumos Online Workbook: Data Interpretation (CCSS: 6.SP.5)**

# Notes

 LumosTestPrep.com

 Lumoslearning

 INCLUDES Online Workbooks!

# About Online Workbooks

- When you buy this book, 1 year access to online workbooks included

- Access them anytime from a computer with an internet connection

- Adheres to the New Common Core State Standards

- Includes progress reports

- Instant feedback and self-paced

- Ability to review incorrect answers

- Parents and Teachers can assist in student's learning by reviewing their areas of difficulty

Course Name: NJ ASK Grade 4 Math Prep

| Lesson Name: | Correct | Total | % Score | Incorrect |
|---|---|---|---|---|
| **Introduction** | | | | |
| Diagnostic Test | | 3 | 0% | 3 |
| **Number and Numerical Operations** | | | | |
| Workbook - Number Sense | 2 | 10 | 20% | 8 |
| Workbook - Numerical Operations | 2 | 25 | 8% | 23 |
| Workbook - Estimation | 1 | 3 | 33% | 2 |
| **Geometry and measurement** | | | | |
| Workbook - Geometric Properties | | 6 | 0% | 6 |
| Workbook - Transforming Shapes | | | | |
| Workbook - Coordinate Geometry | 1 | 3 | 33% | 2 |
| Workbook - Units of Measurement | | | | |
| Workbook - Measuring Geometric Objects | 3 | 10 | 30% | 7 |
| **Patterns and algebra** | | | | |
| Workbook - Patterns | 7 | 10 | 70% | 3 |
| Workbook - Functions and relationships | | | | |

LESSON NAME: Workbook - Geometric Properties

Elapsed Time: 01:19

**Question No. 2**

What type of motion is being modeled here?

**Select right answer**

- ☐ a translation
- ☐ a rotation 90° clockwise
- ◉ a rotation 90° counter-clockwise
- ☐ a reflection

[ Previous question ]  [ Next question ]

---

**Report Name: Missed Questions**

Student Name: Lisa Colbright
Cours Name: NJ ASK Grade 4 Math Prep
Lesson Name: Diagnostic Test

The faces on a number cube are labeled with the numbers 1 through 6. What is the probability of rolling a number greater than 4?

**Answer Explanation**

(C) On a standard number cube, there are six possible outcomes. Of those outcomes, 2 of them are greater than 4. Thus, the probability of rolling a number greater than 4 is "2 out of 6" or 2/6.

| A) | | 1/6 |
|---|---|---|
| B) | | 1/3 |
| C) | Correct Answer | 2/6 |
| D) | | 3/6 |

LumosTestPrep.com

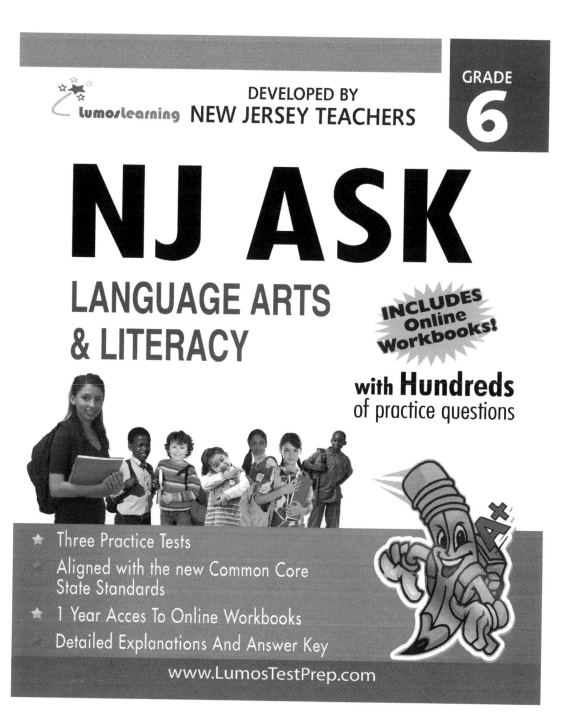

GRADE
6

DEVELOPED BY
NEW JERSEY TEACHERS

lumoslearning

# NJ ASK
## LANGUAGE ARTS & LITERACY

INCLUDES
Online
Workbooks!

with **Hundreds**
of practice questions

★ Three Practice Tests
★ Aligned with the new Common Core State Standards
★ 1 Year Acces To Online Workbooks
★ Detailed Explanations And Answer Key

www.LumosTestPrep.com

# Available
- **At Leading book stores**
- **Online www.LumosTestPrep.com**

Made in the USA
Lexington, KY
24 September 2013